THE QUICK EXPERT'S GUIDE TO

Starting a band

Daniel Gilpin

WAYLAND

First published in 2012 by Wayland

Copyright © Wayland 2012

Wayland
338 Euston Road
London NW1 3BH

Wayland Australia
Level 17/207 Kent Street
Sydney, NSW 2000

Senior editor: Julia Adams
Design: Rocket Design (East Anglia) Ltd
All images and graphic elements: Shutterstock

British Library Cataloguing in Publication Data
Gilpin, Daniel.
Starting a band. -- (Quick expert's guide)
    1. Rock music--Vocational guidance--Juvenile literature.
    2. Bands (Music)--Juvenile literature.
    I. Series
    781.6'6'023-dc23

ISBN 978 0 7502 7052 6

Printed in China

Wayland is a division of Hachette Children's Books,
an Hachette UK company

www.hachette.co.uk

>>>CONTENTS<<<

TO THE UTTERLY EXCELLENT WORLD OF BANDS!

Many people dream about being in a band. They read magazine interviews and rock star biographies just to imagine what it would be like to live that life themselves. Certainly there don't seem to be many lives that are much more glamorous. Playing music to adoring fans seems like a great way to make a living.

The realities of being in a band may not be quite as glitzy as the media would have us believe, but there is no doubt that it is exciting. It can also be massively rewarding, on many different levels. The feeling you get when you first see an audience going wild for a song you wrote is impossible to put into words. It is something that most people never experience. The same goes for the first time you hear your band playing on the radio, or read about yourselves in the press. With the help of our rather excellent guide, you can take the all-important first steps of turning your musical dream into reality.

PLACE YOUR FEET IN THE STARTING BLOCKS AND GET READY FOR THE QUICK EXPERT TEAM'S DEFINITIVE HEAD-START TO STARDOM!

Get tips **straight** from the multi-platinum selling stars...

...who started their bands in their **teens**.

Follow our step-by-step **guide** to promoting your band.

Understand how the music **industry** works.

Get tips on coming up with **original** material for your band.

Find out how to survive the **ups** and **downs** of making music together.

Chapter 1

PREPARATION

So you want to start a band. Where do you begin? Well, before you go and jump in head-first you need to sit down and think. You need to have a clear idea of what you want to achieve before you start setting things in motion. By asking yourself a few important questions now, you will save yourself a lot of bother later on.

✳ INITIAL BRAINSTORM

The first thing to consider is what style of music you want your band to play. When it comes to finding band mates, you'll need to give them some idea of the kind of band you'll be asking them to join. You probably have a good idea already of the kind of sound you're after. How would you describe it? Does it fit into a particular genre — heavy metal, pop, ska, punk, grunge — or are you thinking more of a mixture of styles?

Perhaps there is a particular band or group of bands that play the style of music you want your band to play? Whatever the case, work out the best way to describe what you are after. That way, you are more likely to find like-minded musicians to join your band and avoid potential 'musical differences' later on.

MUSIC GENRES

By and large, music genres are invented by journalists. They are used by people who review and write about bands to group them together, according to the kind of sound they have and the way that they play. That said, once established, genres can be very useful. They can help music fans to discover new bands they otherwise might not have heard of or listened to. And they can help budding band creators like yourself explain to potential band members the sort of music they might be expected to play!

A music genre is invented to describe a kind of music. To someone who had never heard jazz before, the word jazz would be meaningless. But any jazz aficionado could tell you what is jazz and what isn't. The more people listen to and read about a particular genre of music, the more they understand what it is.

Whatever genre of music you are in to and want to play, be it synth-pop or death metal, you are more likely to find people suitable for your band if they smile and understand what you are talking about when you mention that genre's name.

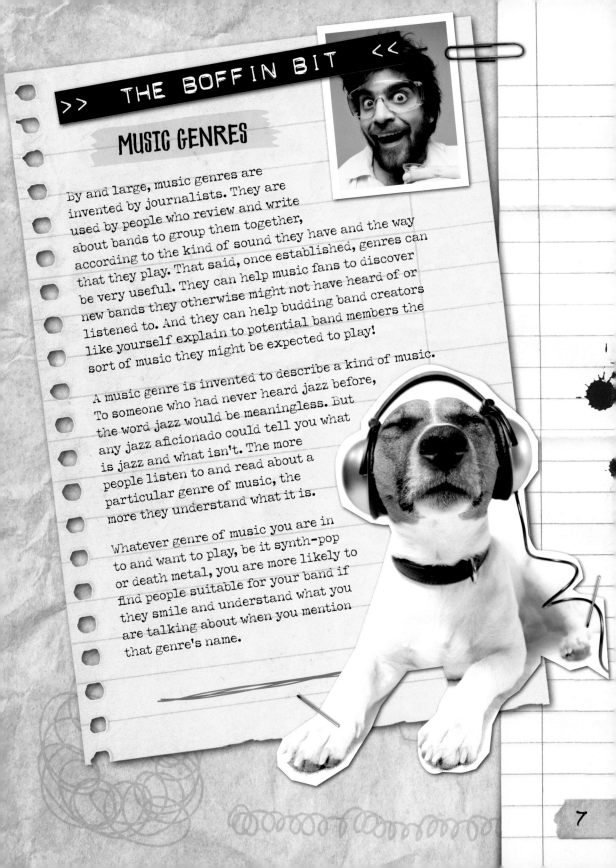

✳ WHO PLAYS WHAT

Once you have settled on a style, you need to think about instrumentation. You can't look for band mates until you know what you need them to play. How many members do you see your band having? Will you be a stripped down trio of guitar, bass and drums, or are you thinking of something bigger? Perhaps you want more than one guitarist, or maybe someone who plays keyboards? What about vocalists? Will you have just one lead singer, or will you need more than one person who can sing? Perhaps most importantly, where do you see yourself in the band? What will you do and how do you see yourself fitting into it?

✳ SONGS AND IMAGE

Another thing to ask yourself is whose songs you see your band playing. Will you write and play your own material or will you do covers? Perhaps you want your band to do a mixture of both. Unless you have some material of your own already, you will probably start off playing cover songs, in your first jam sessions at least. Think about whose songs you want to cover in the early stages of your band. The choices you make now may end up influencing the direction your band takes in the future.

You may well have already thought long and hard about your planned band's music, but it is less likely you will have given much thought to how your band should look. However, the plain fact is that band image is important. The way you look can help you stand out, or identify with fans.

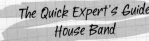

The Quick Expert's Guide House Band

> **"** Being in a band you can wear whatever you want – it's like an excuse for Halloween every day. **"**
>
> **Gwen Stefani**

✳ FINAL THOUGHT

Lastly, you need to think about how serious you are about the whole idea. Do you just want to have fun with your mates or do you want your band to be the next big thing? Although it might not sound it, this is actually a very important question. It is important that you and your future band mates have the same idea about what you are doing. If you are just in it for a laugh and you don't make that clear at the outset, you may end up wasting other people's time. By the same token, if you are dedicated to making the band a success and you don't make that clear, they could end up wasting yours.

GET REAL! Teenagers talk about starting their bands

"I had just finished writing my first songs and all I wanted to do was start a band as soon as possible. I moved to go to college, and of the first five people I met, one of them happened to be a drummer, and one happened to be a guitarist. It was kismet [fate]; we started a band." Chris

"The three of us decided to form the band when we started high school, just as a bit of fun. As we were all beginners we learnt our instruments together." Adam

"I started playing when I was 14. The guitar was the first thing I could do fairly well. About the same time, my neighbour started playing drums. He and I would get together and play every day after school. Soon we realised we needed a bass player. My brother bought a bass and we played our first show." Jason

✳ DON'T STRESS IT!

By now, you might be thinking that you have bitten off more than you can chew. But don't panic, the initial brainstorm is not an exact science. There might be some questions that you cannot answer at the moment, but that doesn't really matter. What does matter is that you do have a really serious think about what you want your band to be before you start launching your idea on other people. The more you can sort out at this stage, the better (although nothing is set in stone — you can always change things later). Put your ideas down on paper, so you don't forget anything, and then get ready for stage two.

Try to come up with an image for your band. Think about the type of music you would like your band to play, then see if you can come up with a suitable look. Bear in mind that a strong, individual image can help you stand out from the crowd. If you can come up with a gimmick that no one else has done before, you could be on to a winner.

The most important things to consider are hairstyles and clothes. A unique hairstyle can make a band's image in it's own right – think of Robert Smith's hair and the image of The Cure, for example. Clothes can either be very uniform and similar, giving the band a cohesive look, or more individual. Often the lead singer will be the most strikingly dressed member of the band, as he or she is usually the main focus of attention for the audience.

Dude!

BE A QUICK EXPERT!

- Before you do anything else, think things through and work out the basics of your band.

- Decide on a style of music. Pick something you like – you will never get anywhere if you don't enjoy what you are doing.

- Work out how many members you will need to make your band. Think about the instruments you will need to make the kind of sound you are after.

- Start thinking about songs. Will you play covers? If so, whose songs will you play?

- Work out an image. How you look will be important to fans.

- Think hard about exactly what you want to achieve with your band. Do you just want to have fun or are you planning to make it big and become stars?

GETTING STARTED

Now you know what you want to achieve, it is time to start turning your idea into reality. Unless you are planning on being a solo artist, the first thing you are going to need is band mates. You may already have one or two people in mind, but it is unlikely that you will already know everyone you will need to make your band complete.

✳ MEET THE BAND

Before you start looking for band mates, you need to work out your requirements. By now, you should have a pretty good idea of how you want your band to sound and look. So what have you got already and what do you need to make the finished article?

The first thing to do is look at your own abilities and see where you will stand (or sit) in the scheme of things. Do you play an instrument or will you sing? Will you write the songs, or are you going to need a songwriter? If you have other people in mind for your band already, what can they play or do that you cannot?

Once you have figured that out, you can work out what other instruments and talents the band will need to create the sound you're after. With that done, you are ready to start looking for new members.

✳ CREATING CHEMISTRY

Most professional musicians would agree that a great band is more than the sum of its parts. It is an entity in its own right, something bigger than the individuals and instruments that make it. The best bands have chemistry, and that comes out in the music they play.

When musicians talk about chemistry, they don't mean the science. They mean the way that band members work together to create the sounds that they do. Good chemistry comes from like-minded people working hard and taking pleasure from the music they create. In a way, it is the energy a band projects. It is what makes watching live band performances so exciting for other people, and what turns gig-goers into fans.

Creating band chemistry isn't easy and it may take a little time, but there are things you can do at this stage that make it more likely to grow. The first, and most important, is to choose people that you like to join your band. You are more likely to enjoy making music with someone you get on with than someone you don't. Potential band members should share your music tastes as well, of course. If they don't, then this is likely to lead to difficulties later on.

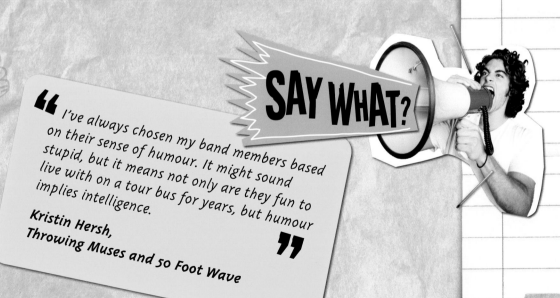

SAY WHAT?

❝ I've always chosen my band members based on their sense of humour. It might sound stupid, but it means not only are they fun to live with on a tour bus for years, but humour implies intelligence. ❞

**Kristin Hersh,
Throwing Muses and 50 Foot Wave**

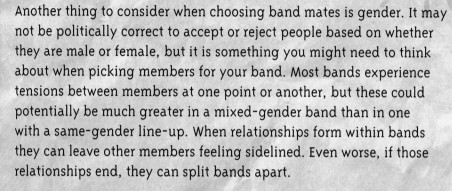

* FUNK SOUL BROTHERS OR SISTERS?

Another thing to consider when choosing band mates is gender. It may not be politically correct to accept or reject people based on whether they are male or female, but it is something you might need to think about when picking members for your band. Most bands experience tensions between members at one point or another, but these could potentially be much greater in a mixed-gender band than in one with a same-gender line-up. When relationships form within bands they can leave other members feeling sidelined. Even worse, if those relationships end, they can split bands apart.

Of course, gender might not be an issue, or might not be one you think will have an impact on your band. If you are in it for the music more than anything else, then finding people you click with on a musical level will probably be the most important thing, regardless of their gender. Many of the most respected and ground-breaking acts and bands have had mixed-gender line-ups — think of The White Stripes, The Pixies, The Kills or The Dears.

Having members of both sexes can also add another element to your band. In terms of vocals, it can help to give your sound greater range. It may also help you to attract a larger fan base. Although many

musicians don't like to admit it, being attractive to guys and girls can increase sales of both merchandise and tickets. Having both male and female band members could work to your advantage on this front.

✳ OTHER THINGS TO CONSIDER

So now you know what you want on a musical and personal level. The next thing to think about is the other stuff that goes with a band. It is all very well having enough guitars and guitarists, but will you have enough amps and other equipment? And what about transport — do you have a car or will you need a band member who does?

All of these other extras are worth considering now. Make a list of all your requirements, so that when you do get around to interviewing potential band members there won't be anything that you forget to ask. You might find it helpful if one or more band members has connections in the music industry, for example. And what about age or previous experience — are these important? If they are, make a note of it now.

✳ HAPPY AS YOU ARE?

You may already have your band in place, or think you do. A lot of bands form almost by accident, by friends getting together and jamming, having fun. In many ways, this is the easiest way to get a band set up, but it is not necessarily the best. Unless all of your friends are very talented, your band may not be as good as some of you might like. And while being in a band can be fun, it can cause friction. Many friendships break up when bands go beyond the jamming stage and start to get more serious.

If you want your band to be more than just a fun hobby it might be worth searching out some serious musicians. (At the very least you should take a look at your current set-up and ask yourself whether your other band members have the same dedication you do.) In many ways, starting a band is like starting a business. If you are in it for the long haul, you want to be in it with partners you can trust — people who will keep their heads if the band suddenly finds success, but who are willing to stick with you through tough times as well.

* NEW BAND MATES — WHERE TO LOOK

If you are serious about finding new band mates, you should cast your net wide. Not too wide however, as you will need to meet up on a regular basis once your band gets going. Think about places locally where musicians go and find out if they have noticeboards or other facilities for putting up small ads. Music shops and gig venues are a good place to start. Visit the ones in your local town (if there are any), then try the nearest city. If you live in a city already then it might just be a matter of hopping on the bus and visiting the venues that you know.

Before you set off, of course, you are going to need a flyer — an advert that you can pin up. Your flyer should contain all the information a potential band member should know — what kind of instrument they should play, the kind of music you see the band playing, and contact details for yourself (an e-mail address is usually best). Perhaps most importantly of all, your flyer should be eye-catching. It needs to stand out from the others on a noticeboard and be the first thing people see.

If your band has a logo, put that on it. Use colour and any images you might think are appropriate to help it stand out from other ads. It goes without saying that you are going to need more than one flyer. Print more copies than you think you will need and take them with you when you set off. Better to come back with a few left over than to run out halfway through.

Try writing an advert for a band mate, to be posted online or pinned up on a bulletin board in a local music shop. Think carefully about the kind of people you want to attract – don't forget to mention age range and the style of music you want your band to play. Try to fit in as much detail as you can while using as few words as possible.

DIY DUDE

Find a band mate!

Dude!

www.craigslist.co.uk

✳ OTHER OPTIONS

As well as posting flyers, you could try advertising online. Sites such as **craigslist, adtrader** and **gumtree** all have sections where musicians can post free adverts to reach out to people in their local area. Just as with a flyer, keep the text straightforward and simple. Make it clear what you are after and don't forget to include your e-mail address.

While you are waiting for people to respond to your adverts, search the same noticeboards and classified ad websites you have used yourself. You may find that there are people already out there who want to join the kind of band you are putting together. On the other hand, there may be other people like you, looking for new members for their band. Unless the vision you have for your band is particularly important to you, you could try contacting them. The worst that can happen is that you don't hit it off and nothing comes of it.

www.adtrader.co.uk

www.gumtree.com

* FIRST CONTACT

Once someone has responded to your advert you need to find out whether they are right for the band. The first thing to do is to ask if they have a demo recording of their singing or playing that you can listen to. This will give you a good idea of whether or not they are up to scratch. If you like what you hear, or if they don't have a demo, the next thing to do is to have a further telephone conversation with them. A phone conversation can tell you a lot and will give you a good idea of whether or not you are likely to hit it off with them in person.

REALITY CHECK

OFFICIAL REALITY CHECKER

THIS CARD CERTIFIES THAT

_ _ _ Melvin _ _ _

IS OFFICIALLY CERTIFIED TO CHECK REALITY ON BEHALF OF THE QUICK EXPERT'S GUIDE

APPROVED

 ## Muse

While some bands are created from people drawn together by adverts, Muse formed in a more traditional way. The band's three members were friends at school – Teignmouth Community College in Devon. In 1994, they entered themselves into a local battle of the bands competition, which they won. "After that," says lead singer Matthew Bellamy, "we started taking ourselves seriously." They began playing gigs and slowly building up a local fan base. Eventually, four years after forming, they released their first EP.

Today, Muse are world famous and critically acclaimed. In August 2012 they performed at the closing ceremony of the London Olympic Games. Their continued success is down to their dedication and their belief in what they do. The fact that they started out as friends has also played a major role in keeping them together.

Once you have spoken on the phone, it is a good idea to ask them to audition. Don't use the word audition — it sounds a bit formal — just ask them if they would like to come round and jam with you and any other band mates you may already have. A jam session will let you see what they can do, and will give you, and them, a good idea of whether you are likely to work well together. If they ask you to go round and see them, take your band mates or a friend, just to be on the safe side. If you have to go on your own, let someone know where you are going and roughly when you expect to get back.

BE A QUICK EXPERT!

- Before you start looking for band mates, work out exactly what part you are going to play in the band yourself.

- If you already have other people who want to join your band, do the same thing with them. Sit down together and work out what part they are going to play.

- When looking for new band mates, make sure you pick people you like. If your band becomes successful, you are going to end up spending a lot of time together with them.

- Think about all the other things you will need for your band. As well as people, you will need equipment. And don't forget to think about things like transport.

WORKING AS A UNIT

By now you may already be dreaming about hitting the big time. But if you are going to make it, there is still a lot more that you need to do. Unless you are planning on being a cover band or a tribute act, you are going to need new material. And once you have got your songs, you are going to have to practise them until they are totally nailed down.

✳ CREATING YOUR SOUND

Think about every band you've ever been into and admired. Chances are, every one of them has performed their own songs. Most bands that become famous hit the big time on the back of a single piece of music. For Coldplay, it was Shiver, for Radiohead, it was Creep.

Writing and performing your own songs helps your band to stand out from the competition. It gives your band its own unique identity — something that is very important to fans. The more you play your own material the more people will get to know it, and the more committed your fans will become. If you are lucky, you too might find yourselves with a hit single on your hands. Everybody likes a song that they can sing along to. Imagine the feeling you will get hearing people sing along to yours.

Writing music isn't easy — at least, not for most people — but the rewards can be immense if you get it right. At the very least, you will have the sense of pride and achievement in having created something new.

✳ COMING UP WITH MATERIAL

If you are going to perform your own music, your band will need a songwriter. That may be you — you may already have one or more songs in the bag. If you don't, you should ask your band mates if they have any songs you could try out. Remember, at this early stage songs don't need to be complete. In fact, many of the best and most famous songs out there came together piece by piece, with different band members trying different things and adding new ideas.

The worst case scenario is that neither you nor any of your band mates has any ideas for songs at all. If that is the case, you have two options — stick to covers until one of you comes up with something, or start looking for a songwriter. Put adverts out just like you did when you were looking for people to join your band.

You may be surprised to learn that there are some people who write songs but cannot play, or who can play but don't want the limelight of performing in a band. We have all heard of Elton John, but how many people have heard of Bernie Taupin? Bernie Taupin wrote the lyrics to practically every one of Elton John's hits. The two of them still work together today.

>> THE BOFFIN BIT <<

SONG ANATOMY

A song is much more than just a list of words and notes strung together. It is a construction made up of several different parts. These parts can be looked at separately and, indeed, can be written separately. However, for a song to be good, they should either flow into one another or follow on from one another in such a way as to be pleasing to the ear.

Most popular songs contain all of the following elements; intro, verse, chorus and outro. Some include other elements, such as a bridge, or an instrumental solo.

As its name suggests, the intro is the first section of a song. Its job is to draw the listener in and build up a feeling of suspense before the song proper begins.

The verse is the main part of a song and usually the first part to appear after the intro. Most songs contain two or more verses, each with the same musical arrangement, but with different lyrics.

The chorus is a section of a song that repeats both musically and lyrically. It is normally the strongest and most memorable part of a song, and is used between verses to link them together.

The outro is the last part of a song. Like the intro, it tends to be instrumental – that is to say, without lyrics. However, unlike the intro, which often takes a completely different musical form, it usually follows on musically from the last verse or chorus.

☀ PRACTICE MAKES PERFECT

Whatever you play, be it covers or your own material, you are going to need to practice to get your band's sound tight. Practicing, or rehearsing, will require your own space. You may be lucky enough to have access to a large room or garage between you, but if you are going to rehearse in a place like this, you need to make sure that the neighbours are understanding people. Alternatively, you could hire out a purpose-made rehearsal space.

Rehearsal spaces usually come in one of two shapes: lockouts, which your band rents exclusively for a month or more at a time, and rehearsal studios, which offer space that can be rented by the hour. Each has its own advantages and disadvantages, as we will see.

Lockouts have the great advantage of being yours and yours alone. In many ways, renting one is a bit like renting your own flat. You pay a fixed amount up front and you then have access to it whenever you like. Because it is your band's space, you can keep all of your band's equipment there. And provided you have enough keys or get enough cut (with the owner's permission), any one or any number of you can go to use it whenever you like.

The disadvantages of lockouts are cost and the lack of equipment provided. Just like flats, rental costs vary greatly depending on where they are, but you should expect to pay at least £150-£400 a month on average. On top of that, you will have to find the money for a PA system, as most lockouts don't provide them. This means a mixer, an amplifier, microphones for every singer, and speakers. These can be rented, but you may find that you end up spending less money if you buy them outright.

Rehearsal studios are a better bet if you are on a tight budget. Because you only rent them by the hour, you can save yourself a lot of rental money every month (most studios cost from £10 to £30 an hour). On top of that, you don't need to spend money on a PA system, as these are always provided. The main disadvantage is that the space is not your own. Other bands use it, limiting the amount of rehearsing you can do. You may find that your studio is booked up more often than you would like, meaning that you and your band cannot always rehearse when you want to.

>> THE BOFFIN BIT <<

THE PA SYSTEM

A PA system is an electronic system for amplifying live sound – making it louder. PA stands for public address: the term was originally used for systems that amplified the human voice for announcements, hence the name. Nowadays, it is also used for the systems used by musicians to amplify the sound of their voices and the instruments they play. Most band PA systems include a mixing console, also known as a mixing desk or mixer, along with the traditional combination of microphones, amplifier and speakers. The mixing console allows the band (or a technician or producer) to alter the volume levels of the various voices and instruments, and may also enable them to add electronic effects to the sounds produced.

✳ KEEPING COSTS DOWN

Whatever option your band goes for, there are ways of saving money. If you rent a lockout, you could try sharing it with another band and splitting the rent between you. If they have a PA system and you manage to convince them to let you use it, you could save yourself even more. (If they are unwilling to share their PA for nothing, try suggesting that your band pays them a small amount of rent to use it.)

Rehearsal studio fees are fixed and cannot be reduced by sharing, as only one band can use a studio at a time. However, you can cut down the amount of time you need to spend in the studio by practicing elsewhere. You can practice on your own at home, of course — headphones are a great way of solving volume problems. And you may find that you can practice with one or more of your band mates in one of your own homes, providing you keep the noise levels down.

✳ BUILD YOUR REPERTOIRE

Now you have got your first songs written and found somewhere to rehearse, it's time to build up your repertoire — in other words, the list of songs that your band can play. Before long, you might be starting to think about playing live. Before you can do that, you need to have enough songs under your belt to last an hour or so on stage.

An hour's worth of your own material may take some time to put together — when you think about it, that's more or less enough to fill an album. While you or your songwriter are working on this, think of covers that your band can play. Sit down with your band mates and discuss this together. You may find that there are songs that you all know already. Or there may be songs some of you really like and want to cover.

Learning to cover other bands' songs is relatively straightforward. The music is already out there, often in written as well as recorded form. You can buy printed songbooks or search for the music and lyrics online. Or you may be the kind of person who can learn a song by ear.

✳ LEARNING TO LISTEN

While you are practicing your chosen cover songs, and your own material, try to listen to your band mates as well as yourself. The more that you learn to listen to each other, the tighter your playing will become and the better your performances will be. Listening to the whole sound will also help you to identify mistakes. If you or a band mate thinks that someone is doing something wrong, stop playing and try to work out what it is together.

Once you have identified the problem, practice that bit until you get it right. If you find listening difficult while playing yourself, try recording your rehearsals and listen to them later. Alternatively, get a friend to come along to your rehearsals and ask them to pick out any mistakes. If you do this, make sure that you choose someone you can trust to be honest. Don't pick a groupie or fan who thinks that everything you ever do is great.

Learning new songs can be frustrating but it is important to keep your cool. Try to be patient — remember that everybody makes mistakes sometimes and perfection takes time! That said, if you find yourselves getting really stuck with a particular song, just leave it for a while and move on to a different one. And bear in mind that your band's original songs are not set in stone. If you or a band mate thinks that something slightly different might sound good, give it a go. Don't let the songwriter be too precious about his or her creation.

✳ MAKING SET LISTS

Before you start playing live you need to think about making some set lists. A set list is simply a list of songs in a particular order, to be played at a live performance. Of course, live performances vary in length, so you should have set lists of different length, too. Before you start thinking about looking for gigs, you should put together set lists of 15 minutes, 30 minutes, 45 minutes and an hour.

When you are arranging your set lists, bear in mind that you should always start and finish strong. Put what you think are your best songs at the beginnings and ends of each list. Creating set lists will give you an idea of how much material you actually have, and whether you can really consider playing longer gigs just yet.

Once you have got your set lists ready, practice them to find out how long they actually last, then add a little bit of time to account for talking and tuning your instruments between songs. You might want to record these practice sessions, too. Listening back, you can work out which song combinations work best. You might also find that one of your recordings is good enough to be used later as a demo.

SAY WHAT?

❝ The band set up... and just started rehearsing. If there was a song, we'd just rehearse it as a band, and it would get arranged as a band, and it got changed around a lot. ❞

James Iha, The Smashing Pumpkins and A Perfect Circle

✳ TIME FOR A SERIOUS TALK

Writing songs and rehearsing is all part of the fun of being in a band. Working together creatively in this way is almost a reward in itself and, if you play your cards right, it can lead to much bigger and better things later on.

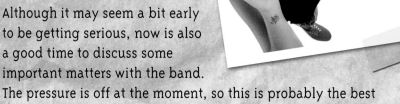

Although it may seem a bit early to be getting serious, now is also a good time to discuss some important matters with the band. The pressure is off at the moment, so this is probably the best time to get them out of the way.

The first thing to consider now is how decisions will be made within the band. This may not sound important, but getting this out of the way now could save a lot of arguing later on. Will you make band decisions democratically, each casting a vote to decide on important matters, or will you let the big decisions be made by just one or two particular band members? Whatever model you decide to go with, make sure that everyone in the band understands and agrees on it now.

✳ MONEY MATTERS

The second thing to think about is the all important question of money. If you do ever make any, how are you going to split the profits? Will you divide them up evenly, or will the singer or songwriter get a larger cut? Bear in mind that income from different sources can be divided up in different ways. For example, you could split the money made from live performances evenly, but give the songwriter a higher percentage of the earnings from downloads and CD sales.

The flip-side of the money question is perhaps even more pertinent at the moment. By now, you will have already started spending money on the band — buying equipment, or paying for rehearsals, for example. You need to think about setting aside some of your earnings to pay for band expenses in the future.

The best way to do this is to set up a bank account for the band. If you have a manager or band member you all trust enough, you could get that person to open and manage the account in their own name. That person would then also be responsible for accessing and spending the money when needed. A better, and safer, solution is to legally register your band as a business. That way, you can open a business bank account in the band's name. If you are all cosignatories (if you all put your names down when opening it), you will all be able to keep an eye on the account, even if you decide that only one of you should be responsible for managing it and spending money from it. Having a band bank account helps you to keep tabs on what you are spending, or making, as a band. While you are still in the spending stage, you will all need to put money into it. Hopefully, it won't be long before you start drawing money out.

✳ I'LL HAVE THAT IN WRITING

You might want to get a lawyer to draw up a contract regarding what you decide to do about money in the band. That way, it all becomes official and everyone involved is protected. If this sounds a bit scary and grown-up, remember that most bands end up signing legal contracts at some point or another. By drawing one up now together with a lawyer, you will all be less daunted by the prospect of reading through and signing contracts later on.

✳ LOOKING AHEAD

Money and band politics are serious matters. It's good to get them sorted out while the band is still relatively new. Another, less weighty matter to discuss is the band's plan of action. This involves setting goals for you and your band mates to aim for in the future.

Sit down together and ask yourselves where you see the band in three months time. Then think about where you see the band in six months and a year from now.

Three month goals to aim for might include having a regular practice schedule in place, building your repertoire to a certain number of songs, or playing your first live show. By six months, you might expect to have recorded a demo CD and be playing live shows on a regular basis. In a year's time, you might have started your first tour, have a record contract, and be living off your music.

These are all just ideas and the timings may well vary for your band. However, setting goals like these will help to give your band structure and focus. If you don't start out with an idea of where you want the band to go, it may not end up actually going anywhere at all.

✳ NAMING YOUR BAND

The one thing we haven't talked about yet in this chapter is the one thing you may have put a lot of thought into already — what to call your band. A band's name is an important part of its image. It can say a lot about the kind of music you play — Napalm Death, for instance, is a heavy sounding name and you would expect a band called Napalm Death to play heavy sounding music. On the other hand, a band's name may say very little about its music, or nothing at all. The most important thing is for your band name to be memorable and to be something that you are all happy with. After all, you may have to live with it for the rest of your lives.

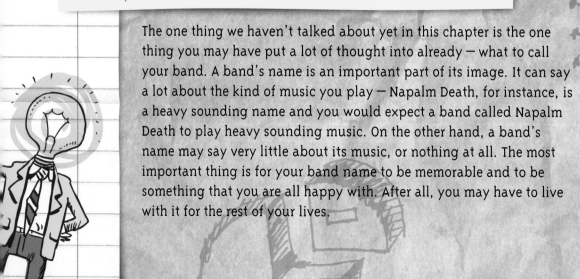

Try to come up with a list of possible names for your band. You may have an idea for a band name already, but as you don't know yet whether or not your other band mates will like it, it might be useful to have a few alternatives up your sleeve. Think of bands you like and try to work out what it is that makes their names memorable. And keep a couple of simple rules in mind as you try to come up with ideas.

First of all, make sure that your band names are easy to spell. When you start selling your music online, you want people searching for it to be able to find it easily. By the same token, it is a good idea to make your band names sound unique. If you use everyday words or word combinations they may become lost in the mass of internet search results. Unusual words and word combinations are also more likely to stick in a listener's head. If someone hears a song they like on the radio for the first time, they are more likely to remember who it was by if the band had an unusual name.

Once you have your names, check that there are no other bands using them already. The easiest way to do this is to type them into Google or another search engine and see what comes up.

Dude!

BE A QUICK EXPERT!

- Unless you are planning on being a cover band, try writing new material. Ask your band mates for their ideas, too. They may already have songs of their own that they want to try out.

- If you find yourselves stuck for ideas, try looking for a songwriter. There are people out there who write songs but have no interest in playing in a band.

- Decide among yourselves how big decisions will be made within the band and work out how any money that the band makes will be split between its members.

PLAYING LIVE

You've got your sound and image sorted, and you've put your first set lists together. You've practised hard and you know all of your band's songs by heart. Now it's time to take yourselves out of the garage or rehearsal room and start playing live.

✳ SMALL BEGINNINGS

Playing live for the first time can be a daunting experience. If possible, it is a good idea to let yourselves in gently. Try organising a small gig to play for your friends, or offer to play a set at a friend's party. That way, the audience may already know some of your songs and they are more likely to forgive any slip-ups or mistakes.

Playing small gigs to friends is a good way for your band to build up confidence. It can also help to keep costs down, especially if you are playing at someone else's house. As well as being great fun, you can think of it as 'live practice'.

SAY WHAT?

❝ When we started this band all we ever wanted to do was write songs that meant something to us and play them live for as many people as we possibly could, and now in our old age all we want is exactly the same thing. ❞

Frank Iero, My Chemical Romance

With two or three of these gigs under your belt you will be better prepared for playing live in front of an audience that doesn't know you. (That said, you can always invite friends along to later gigs. Friendly faces in the audience always help calm down nerves.)

✳ DO IT YOURSELF

As long as you have a house or garden big enough, organising your own concert should be relatively easy. Before you start, make sure that you have understanding neighbours, and let them all know what you are planning beforehand — no one wants their first gig closed down by the police! Plan your gig for the weekend — Friday or Saturday are best. That way you can play a bit later without worrying about disturbing people who might need to get up and go to work the next morning.

Your guests may come to hear you play, but while they are there they will want refreshment. Make sure that you provide some, or ask them to bring their own. If you know any other bands, you could invite them to come along and play too. Doing this will both increase the size of your audience and allow you to play a shorter set if you want.

✳ SOMEONE ELSE'S PARTY

Playing at someone else's event can be even cheaper than organising your own. You don't need to worry about providing refreshment for a start. If you know somebody who has got a birthday or other special event coming up, try suggesting your band as entertainment at their party. As long as you point out that you will play for free, bring your own equipment and clear up after yourselves, you should have no problem convincing them that it's a good idea.

✳ THE NEXT STEP

Playing gigs for friends is one way to get started but it is not something you have to do. Many bands miss it out entirely and go straight to the next step — playing live in front of an audience of strangers. When you are starting out, the best way to get to do this is to play at an open mic night — an evening entertainment event where anyone can perform. Many pubs and other small venues put these on. Like playing for friends, they are a good way to practice and hone your band's live skills. Finding them is fairly easy too: just do an online search for 'open mic night' together with the name of your nearest city or town.

✳ PLAYING TO WIN

Open mic nights have a lot going for them — for one thing, they are free. If you are prepared to spend a little bit of money however, another option is to play a talent show or battle of the bands. These usually require you to pay an entrance fee, but often offer cash prizes that would more than cover your costs.

As well as offering the potential of making a bit of money, they are very good places to make new contacts in the music industry — not least other bands, who you may want to meet up with and play with in the future. As they are often covered by the local press, they are also a good way to get your band better known, particularly if you are good enough to win or reach the finals.

DEDICATED MUSIC VENUES

Once you have got a few open mic performances under your belt, or if you do well in a talent show or battle of the bands, you should be in a position to approach music clubs and other venues. Make sure that you keep evidence of your success or past performances (such as flyers or press cuttings), as these will be helpful in convincing venue owners to give you a go.

When you are trying to get your band booked for the first time, be realistic about the size of the venues you choose. There is no point going straight for the biggest club in town. Start small and be prepared to work your way up. Be prepared to play for small fees (or even for free) as well. At this stage it is most important to build a fan base and get your band known. Making lots of money will come along later (if you are lucky).

DIY DUDE

Promote your gig!

Whether you are organising your own show or playing at an established venue, you are not going to pull in the punters in unless you promote yourselves. Try designing a poster or flyer to advertise your band's performance. Do a quick image search online for 'band posters' and 'band flyers' to get some ideas, then sketch out a rough layout by hand.

Make sure that your band's name features prominently in the design and don't forget to include the all important (although, at this stage, possibly imaginary) details of where and when you will be playing, how much tickets cost and where or how people can buy them.

Dude!

KEEP ON KEEPING ON

Another thing to be prepared for is being ignored or, worse, being rejected. Most music venues receive an almost continuous list of requests for bookings. If you find that no one is responding to your requests, keep on trying. Often, getting a booking is simply a question of being the loudest and most persistent voice. Follow up on your initial contact with a phone call, and if you get fobbed off, try again later. If a venue turns you down, don't be disheartened. You can always come back and try them later when you are a bit better known.

THE GREAT OUTDOORS

Nowadays, live music is about more than just clubs. Another great way to get your band out there and build your fan base is to start playing festivals. Music festivals come in all sorts of shapes and sizes, from small local events to huge spectaculars, such as Glastonbury. As a new band, you may find that festival promoters are more open to your requests to play than traditional venue owners are. Many sell tickets not only on the back of big headline acts, but also on the number of bands they have playing in their line ups. Again, be prepared to play for little if any money at all. And if you do get to play, make sure that the audience knows who you are. When you stop between songs to thank them, make sure you mention your band's name. Or wear t-shirts or put up a banner with your band's name printed on it. That way, when your new fans get home they will know who to search for online, and who to recommend to their friends.

✳ GO IN WITH YOUR EYES OPEN

Wherever you play your first shows there are a few things to keep in mind. First of all, you may not make any money, in fact, you may even make a loss. This is normal, so don't worry. Just make sure that you have some band savings in place before you start out. Secondly, don't forget to promote your band whenever you play. Use posters, flyers, social network sites (such as Facebook), and word of mouth. If you don't tell people that you are going to be performing you cannot really expect anyone to turn up. Lastly, be wary of 'pay to play' venues. These places will ask you for money up front, and unless you are really confident of selling lots of tickets, your band savings could disappear in no time at all.

BE A QUICK EXPERT!

- Make your first live performance as stress-free as possible. Organise a small gig for friends or arrange to play at a friend's party. That way, you can be guaranteed a fairly supportive and understanding audience.

- Don't worry if your first performance is not all you had hoped. Playing live is an art that takes a little bit of time to perfect. The more practice you get, the better you will become at it.

- Try open mic nights. These are a good, inexpensive way to get your band noticed.

- Be prepared to play for free or very little money to begin with. You can't expect to sell many tickets or command high fees until you have some experience and an established following behind you. Building a fan base takes time.

RECORDING AND PROMOTION

Playing live can help cement a band together, but it can only take you so far. If you want to get your sound out to a wider audience you are going to need to record at least some of your tracks.

✳ THE DEMO

The first thing that most bands record is a demo CD. This is a recording made for sending to people in the music industry, in order to give them an idea of what a band sounds like.

A good demo should include just three or four songs. When planning your demo, pick the best songs that you have. Unless you are a cover band, avoid including covers — all of your songs should be original. Try to make sure that the first song on the demo takes no more than 30 seconds to get to the chorus or hook — people in the music industry get sent masses of demos, and if they are not sucked in straight away they may just skip to the next song or, even worse, switch off. It is vital to get their attention early.

If possible, make that first song your very best one, too. Follow it with your second best song, then your third best one, and so on. Remember that even if they think you are good, many industry people will not bother listening to your demo all the way through.

✳ HELP AND PREPARATION

These rules are important, but being as familiar with and attached to your songs as you probably are, you may not be able to decide which ones are the best. If this is the case, try asking someone you trust who has heard you play before for their opinion. Or, if you have already played live a few times, try to remember which songs got the biggest reaction from the audience. Chances are, if your audiences liked one or two songs more than the others, a music executive or journalist is going to as well.

Once you have chosen the songs for your demo you should plan some extra rehearsal time to make sure that you all know them inside out. When the time comes to record them, your band should be able to perform the songs effortlessly. A demo is about making that all important first impression, and the more professional and tight you sound on it, the more likely it is to have the desired effect. It is also good to sound driven and passionate, so try to make sure that you enjoy what you are doing. If you are starting to get a bit fed up with any of the songs that will be going on your demo, do your best to hide it when it comes to actually recording them!

> **"** If people are really excited about their music, and that's their primary motivation, then that comes through in [their] demo. That's the most important ingredient. **"**
>
> **Greg Ginn, owner of SST Records**

SAY WHAT?

✳ RECORDING THE DEMO

For your demo to be successful, the most important factors by far are the songs you choose to put on it and how well you perform them. However, recording quality can also make a bit of a difference. Sit down with your band and discuss how much you are willing to spend on the recording process. If you are serious about getting your demo right, it is worth going for the most expensive option you can afford. (Bear in mind that you could also sell your demo to your fans as an EP.)

Once you have set a budget you will be able to consider the options. The first and most obvious one is to book a block of time in a recording studio. While this may cost a bit, you will be recording in a purpose-built space with good quality equipment laid on. Some studios are more expensive than others, of course. The more affordable ones can be rented for as little as £25 an hour, but others may be as much as £90 an hour, or even more.

Another option is to go for home studio recording. With technology being what it is today, a one-off investment of a few hundred pounds can buy you enough equipment to record straight onto your computer. The advantage of this, of course, is that once you have the equipment you can use it over and over again. If you later decide that you want to record another EP or an album you can do it yourself for free. Alternatively, you could pay to use somebody else's home studio equipment. This would almost certainly be cheaper than renting space in a professional recording studio.

The third and cheapest option is to record yourselves in your rehearsal space with a portable audio recorder. Digital recorders are quite affordable, ranging upward from around £30. A digital recorder is preferable to an old-fashioned tape recorder, as you will need to transfer your music to a computer in order to burn CDs. Most people in the music industry expect demos to arrive on CD nowadays.

THE MASTERING PROCESS

Once you have recorded your band's demo, it is a good idea to get it mastered. Mastering both enhances the sound quality and increases the volume of a recording, so that when it is played back it has a sound that can compete with commercial CDs. In order to get your recording mastered, you will have to take it to a sound engineer, who will expect to be paid. However, this money will be money well spent. A mastered demo can be reproduced on CD over and over, and makes a quality product that you can sell to fans at gigs or by mail order through your band's website.

MAKING A PRESS KIT

The demo is vital if you want to get yourselves heard by other people in the music industry. However, it is only one part of the press kit you should send them. Along with the CD itself, you should include a cover letter, a band photo and a band bio. You should also include copies of any press clippings you may have (these can include sections of online articles). Rather than printing out and including these clippings individually, try to cut them out and arrange them on a single sheet, which can then be photocopied.

The demo CD you send with your press kit should be plain and have the name of your band, the song titles, and your contact details written clearly on it. If you have a band website, include its web address too. Avoid the temptation to cover the demo CD with artwork: save this for the copies you intend to sell to fans instead.

The cover letter should be personalised for every individual that you send your press kit to. Rather than 'Dear Sir or Madam' or 'To whom it may concern', use their name after the word 'Dear' at the beginning. Print it on good quality paper (that goes for all of the material in your press kit) and include your contact information at the top. If you have a band logo, use that as a letterhead.

✳ LOOKING THE PART

Your band photo should be a 20 × 25 cm (8 × 10 in) colour or black and white image showing your band looking as cool as possible. Consider hiring a professional photographer to do your shoot. If that sounds a bit too expensive, ask a friend or relative with a good camera and a bit of photographic knowledge to do it for you.

Make sure that you all wear outfits that reflect your band's image and pick a good location for the background. When it comes to selecting the picture to use, choose one that shows all of your faces clearly. Do not use a shot from a live performance, as these rarely show much detail of how bands really look.

It's all about geek-chic, people!

WHAT IS A BAND BIO?

Well, bio is actually short for biography. Your band bio is basically the story of your band. It contains all the information that someone who has never seen or heard your band should know.

A band bio should be short and get straight to the point. Try to make yours no more than three paragraphs long. Use the first paragraph to get all of the most important information out of the way. It is here that you should mention the style of music you play and other bands you think you may sound like, as well as the name of your band and where you are from.

Use the other paragraphs to explain who is in the band and what they play, and to give the reader a little bit of background into the band's history. Mention any significant accomplishments, but don't exaggerate. Don't say that you play all sorts of styles, or that you don't fit into any musical genre. If you are not sure what or who you sound like, ask a trusted friend. People who read band bios want to get an idea of what a band is, not what it isn't.

The final thing to consider adding to your press kit is a fact sheet with bullet points, showing your list of accomplishments. These may include competitions won, impressive sales figures and a list of venues played. Omit the fact sheet altogether if you are a new band or one yet to amass much experience.

Make sure that everything you include in your press kit has your contact information on it. Things get separated, but you want anyone you send your press kit to to be able to get back to you, whatever part of it they have to hand.

✳ ONLINE PRESENCE

The internet is a great promotional tool. Unlike traditional advertising, it has the great advantage of being virtually free. On top of that, it is interactive. People use it to buy music, or listen to clips. And it allows fans to get closer to their favourite bands and artists, or at least feel like they are.

Once you have started playing live and recorded a demo, it makes sense to build an online presence for your band. There are several ways that you can do this. If you have the time, you should try to do as many of them as possible.

✳ FREE-TO-USE SITES

The first thing most bands do is create a page on **MySpace**. MySpace is almost custom-made for bands. It allows you to upload pictures, text and music, and create a place where fans can visit to keep up with your band news.

The next thing to do is create a page for your band on the social media websites. **Facebook** and **Bebo** are the best known of these. Once your page is up and running, invite friends to 'Like' it.

Use the word 'official' in brackets after your band name for the title of your page, so that fans know it's you and not someone else pretending to be you.

Other websites worth investigating include **Wikipedia** and **Twitter**. Wikipedia will allow you to create your own entry (page) for your band, providing you follow the site rules. Twitter can be useful for keeping your fans updated with band news. It can also make fans feel more like they are part of the band, helping to increase their loyalty.

YOUR OWN BAND WEBSITE

As well as taking advantage of all the free online promotional options available to you, it is well worth considering setting up a band website of your own. Although your own website may cost you a little to create and then host, it can end up making you money in the long run. You can use your own website to sell your music and other band merchandise, and because you own it yourselves you will not have to pay anybody else commission. A band website is also a great way to project your image. Unlike MySpace and Facebook you have complete control over its design. Read **The Quick Expert's Guide to Building a Website** to find out more.

Search for your favourite bands on MySpace, Facebook and Bebo. Have a look at their official pages and think about how they use these websites to promote themselves. What you discover may come in useful when the time comes to create your own band pages.

DIY DUDE

Web presence

✳ GET NOTICED

With press kit made and website up and running, you are now in a position to get your band noticed by more people who have never heard of you before. Send your press kit to larger venues that you might not yet have played. And send copies to bigger bands that you know of and admire — they may end up getting back to you with an offer to support them at a big gig or on tour.

As with all promotion, remember to follow up these first contact attempts with a phone call to show that you are keen. Your press kit is more likely to be read and your demo listened to if you do this than if you just stick it in the post and hope.

✳ THE MUSIC PRESS

The other people to send your press kit to are the music press, of course. When contacting them, avoid using the word 'demo' to describe the CD you have sent them. If you mention it at all in your cover letter or other literature, call it your first EP instead. That way, it is more likely to end up being listened to and possibly reviewed by the music journalists you target.

When sending out your press kit, try to avoid being a music snob. Don't just send it to the magazines or papers you may read and respect, send it to everyone you can think of. Don't forget to send copies to the local press and music review websites (such as **indiemusicreviewer.com** and **pitchfork.com**) too. Remember, you are trying to get your band known. It doesn't really matter where people hear about you first. What matters is that they hear about you at all.

✳ RADIO PLAY

For many bands, getting played on the radio is like the Holy Grail. It is the one thing they seek above all else. Radio play is certainly useful and a great way to get your songs heard by new listeners. But it is not something you should sit back and hope will happen — instead you should make it happen yourself.

Treat radio stations in the same way that you treat the music press. Send your press kit with 'debut EP' to any DJs you think might be interested.

Again, don't be too selective about who you send it to. Send to the big names by all means, but don't forget the smaller independent and local stations, too. Even pirate stations are worth targeting, if you can get their addresses!

BE A QUICK EXPERT!

- Get your sound out there by recording a demo. Pick your best three or four songs to go on it and put the best one of all first.

- Before recording, make sure that you have got your songs totally nailed down. Keep rehearsing until everyone in your band knows the songs for your demo inside out.

- Make a press kit to send out to people in the music industry. As well as your demo, this should include a cover letter, a band bio and a photo of the band.

- Use the internet to promote your band. Take advantage of free-to-use sites and think about creating your own band website.

Chapter 6

TAKING IT TO THE NEXT LEVEL

Being in a band can be great fun, but if you want to make sure that it stays that way, it is important to take care of the serious stuff too. If your band is successful, it could make a lot of money. How much of that money ends up in your bank account, rather than lining the pockets of others, will depend on decisions made by you and your band's other members while you are still making a name for yourselves.

✳GETTING A MANAGER

There is one band member we have barely mentioned so far. That person is the one the public rarely sees and the one few people outside the industry ever think about — the band manager. A good manager can make the difference between a band hitting the big time or fading away into obscurity. Providing you have got talent, with the right person behind you the sky's the limit.

That said, of course, band managers don't work for nothing. Typically, a manager will take a cut of around 10-15 per cent of the band's earnings, and if you are not already making serious money they might expect to be paid a fee up front. For that, they will take care of the band's business affairs, managing your money to make sure that things run smoothly and using their contacts in the industry to hook you up with new opportunities (such as recording contracts). They will also do their best to promote you, particularly if they are working for a percentage of your earnings, rather than a fee. Normally, they would be listed as the contact person in your press kit.

BAND MANAGEMENT SOFTWARE

Band management software makes it easier to manage your band yourself. It can help you keep tabs on your band's income and expenditure, as well as sell merchandise and book up live performances. Among the best known packages are **MyBandLink** and **Indie Band Manager,** but there are many others.

While band management software can save you time, it will not have all the contacts and industry knowledge a real professional manager will have. Before you go out and spend money on it, consider whether software or a real manager would be better for your band.

✳ GOING IT ALONE

You may have already decided that you want to manage your band yourself. If you have contacts in the music industry and a good head for business, this may seem like the most sensible idea. However, once things start getting busy, you may want to change your mind. Band managers exist for a reason. It can become difficult to find the time to rehearse, play gigs and manage the business side of a band all at once, particularly if you also have a regular day job to pay the bills (and most people who play in up and coming bands do). If you do decide to manage the band yourself, it may be worth investing in some band management software. This can help to cut down on the headaches and free up some of your time.

The third option is to get a friend or relative to manage your band. While this should work out cheaper than hiring a professional manager, you will need to be sure that they are both competent and dedicated to your band's success.

✳ MUSIC AGENTS

Once you appoint a manager, that person becomes part of the life of the band. Another type of person that you (or your manager) may have regular contact with is the music agent. Music agents book and help promote shows. They liaise with venue owners to arrange dates and organise all of the other details that go along with any live performance.

>> THE BOFFIN BIT <<

BAND CONTRACT

If you take on a manager or an agent you will need to sign a contract. This will set out exactly what the manager or agent will do for the band – in essence, it will be their job description. Make sure that you read the contract thoroughly before you sign it. If you have any questions or if there are things that you don't understand, just ask.

Most managers and agents will be willing to alter their contracts to accommodate your wishes – if, for example, there is something that you will want them to do for the band that is not already mentioned. If the idea of legal contracts scares you, contact a lawyer. They will go through the contract with you and answer any questions you may have.

Music agents can also book up and organise tours. They make their money by taking a cut of the earnings from the live performances they work on. This is typically around 10 per cent, but may be more, depending on their reputation. As well as removing all of the hassle of arranging and promoting live shows, a good agent can end up making your band money. Because of the way that they are paid, it is in their interest to make sure that your live performances are successful. They use their knowledge to make sure that you play at bigger venues and to larger audiences than you would manage if you were booking gigs yourself.

CD SALES

Once your band is established, you can start to expect to be paid for playing live. However, even before you get this far you can make a bit of money by selling your CD at gigs, or online.

As has already been mentioned, you can try selling your demo CD to fans. If you are going to do this it is worth making your CD look professional. Create some artwork for the front and back covers and the disc itself, or commission a local artist or graphic designer to do it for you.

You can then use this, together with your digital music files, to create a booklet, disc and back cover using the product templates from a service such as **Cafe Press**. Alternatively, you can contact a professional service such as **Disc Makers** or **Disc Factory** and ask them to do it for you. The cases for your CDs can be bought online.

If your budget is really tight, you can use a CD burner to create a small run of CD-Rs yourself. The disadvantage is that they will not look professionally produced and a lot of potential customers will be put off from buying them. Bear in mind that most professional services will also supply you with CD-Rs (although with more professional-looking printing) unless you order a significant quantity of copies (usually 1,000 or more).

www.cafepress.co.uk

www.discmakers.co.uk

www.discfactory.co.uk

You may well have enough material to fill an entire album. If this is the case, and you decide to record it, it is definitely worth shelling out enough for 1,000 professionally produced CDs. As with your demo ('first EP'), do everything you can to promote your album. Send copies, with your press kit (minus the demo CD), to everyone you can think of in the music, national and local press who might review it. And always take along more copies than you think you will need to every gig you play. Better to bring some home than to sell out early.

✳ OTHER MERCHANDISE

Anyone who has ever been to a gig knows that bands try to sell more than just CDs. Fans like to buy all sorts of items, from the obvious, such as t-shirts and posters, to the more obscure, such as mugs and keyrings. If you have artwork for your CD you will probably also have a band logo. If not, you should create one, or get someone to design one for you. This can then be printed on whatever you want to sell (as can your album cover).

Websites such as **Cafe Press** and **Zazzle** can be used to make up small numbers of items. This is worth trying first, to find out how well (or not) your merchandise will sell. Once you have established that you have got a market you should then use professional services and order in bulk. This will reduce your costs and increase the profit margin on everything you sell.

✳ SELL, SELL, SELL

Once your name and logo become known you have effectively become a brand. As a musician, you might not like the thought of this, but the fact is you need to embrace it. If you don't take control of how your name and image makes money, somebody else will.

Selling your music and merchandise nowadays is a lot easier than it was in the past. With the rise in online shopping, you can now reach customers in virtually every corner of the globe. You should take advantage of this by using your band website to sell your products, but you should not confine yourself to this channel alone. There are all sorts of other websites that will allow you to sell your merchandise, in exchange for a small percentage fee. The best known are **eBay** and **Amazon**. Both of these are well worth exploring. Others include **CD Baby** and **Play.com**. You can even sell through **MySpace**.

Of course, as musicians you can sell more than just physical merchandise. You can use your band website to allow fans to download music, for a price. Other websites will also help to sell your music downloads for you. You should try **CD Baby** first — their digital distribution deal means that your music will also appear for sale via **iTunes** and other music download services.

www.cdbaby.com

✳ GETTING SIGNED

Once upon a time, you were nobody until you were signed. Getting a record contract was the only way to get your music heard by the wider world. Nowadays, of course, all that has changed. Many bands do perfectly well on their own, without ever signing to a record label.

That said, being with a label can have some advantages. Much of the effort involved in promoting your band and selling your music is taken out of your hands, leaving you more time to concentrate on the music itself — and the rock and roll lifestyle, of course! Getting signed can mean financial security and having the time to properly think through and record an album. But it can also be a decision you later regret.

If you ever do find yourselves in the position to join a label, make sure that you go through the contract with a fine tooth comb before signing it. And show it to a lawyer before you commit.

Just like music, record labels are many and varied. The best known are the 'majors' — companies such as **Sony Music** and **EMI**. Many smaller labels are actually fully- or partly-owned subsidiaries of these giants: **Parlophone** and **Positiva Records** are both owned by EMI, for example. Other smaller record labels are completely independent. If you are thinking about getting signed, do some research to find out which label or labels might be right for you.

First of all, have a think about the kind of music you make. Do you write 'hits' and do you have a popular, marketable image? If not, then there will already be some labels you can strike off your list. Have a look at bands that you or your fans might consider to be like yourselves, and find out which labels they are signed to (if they are signed at all). Buy a label directory book or do a bit of research on the internet.

SAY WHAT?

❝ For new bands, I think a major label is the safest place to be. Independent labels are the ones getting away with murder. A lot of them are hobbyists who rip off young bands, taking advantage of people who would never get signed to a major. ❞

Jack White

Once you have chosen the labels you think might be right for you, contact the person listed by them as 'A&R'. Once you start getting replies, stay cool. Don't just sign up to anything. Make sure that the label is offering you a deal that you can live with, and get a lawyer to check the contract over before you put pen to paper. Remember, once you have signed a record contract you are legally locked in.

✳ MUSIC PUBLISHING

If you are the band's songwriter or lyricist, then music publishing is another avenue you can go down to make money. Songwriters and lyricists automatically own the copyright to the songs or lyrics they create (except in the United States, where copyright has to be registered). Music publishing is a way of exploiting that copyright for monetary gain.

The most common arrangement is for a songwriter or lyricist to make a deal with a music publisher, essentially signing away part of their copyright (usually 50 per cent) in return for the services of that publisher in exploiting the copyright. Music publishers do this by using their connections to place songs in compilation albums, film scores, television programmes, adverts and so on. They then collect the royalties, which are split between the songwriter or lyricist and themselves.

Music publishing can be particularly lucrative for songwriters and lyricists. If you manage to land the contract to soundtrack a major advert, for example, you can expect to be paid very handsomely indeed. On top of that, your song will get massive exposure, being streamed into the living rooms of every home in the country, and sometimes many other countries too. This can give a huge boost to single and album sales. Some artists and bands have even made their names through getting their songs played on adverts.

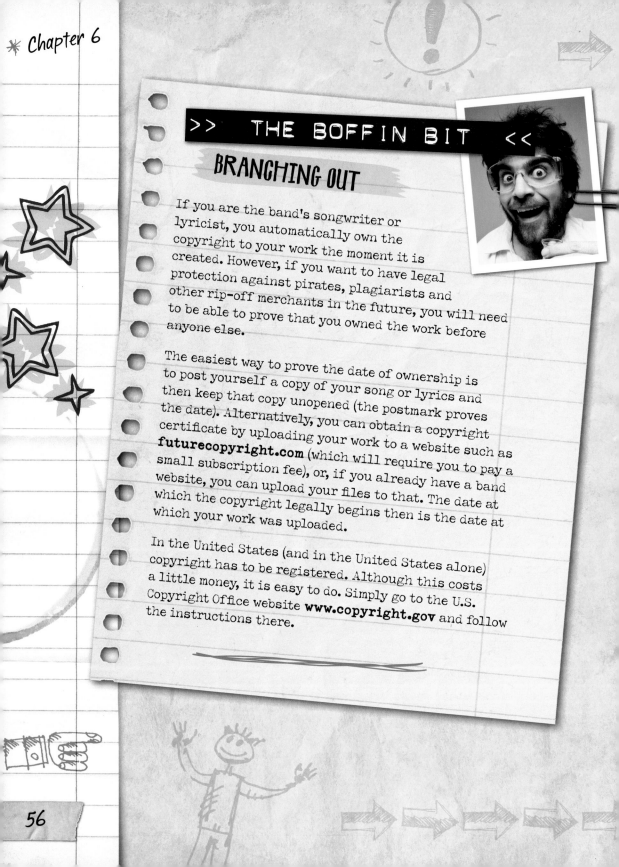

>> THE BOFFIN BIT <<

BRANCHING OUT

If you are the band's songwriter or lyricist, you automatically own the copyright to your work the moment it is created. However, if you want to have legal protection against pirates, plagiarists and other rip-off merchants in the future, you will need to be able to prove that you owned the work before anyone else.

The easiest way to prove the date of ownership is to post yourself a copy of your song or lyrics and then keep that copy unopened (the postmark proves the date). Alternatively, you can obtain a copyright certificate by uploading your work to a website such as **futurecopyright.com** (which will require you to pay a small subscription fee), or, if you already have a band website, you can upload your files to that. The date at which the copyright legally begins then is the date at which your work was uploaded.

In the United States (and in the United States alone) copyright has to be registered. Although this costs a little money, it is easy to do. Simply go to the U.S. Copyright Office website **www.copyright.gov** and follow the instructions there.

✳ GOING ON TOUR

In many ways, going on tour is the ultimate band experience. Nothing else really compares with it. Some musicians love going on tour, others hate it. Either way, it is something nearly all successful musicians have to do. Nowadays, most bands earn more money from live performances than from single or album sales.

Going on tour is basically playing live to as many different audiences as possible in a particular number of days, weeks or months, and in the process selling as many tickets as you can. It is hard work, but it can also be incredibly good fun. If you are already an established name, it can make you rich. If you are still up and coming, it can help you break new ground and bring your music to the attention of a whole new set of fans.

The size of tour you undertake will depend on the financial resources of your band. If you are signed to a record label, they may organise a tour for you, and take care of all the promotion and other arrangements. If your band is not signed, you will have to do it all yourselves. In this case, consider hiring a booking agent. He or she will be able to use their knowledge to save you money in all sorts of ways, and at the same time book venues that are appropriate in size and potential audience make up for your band.

Before considering a tour, make sure that everyone is truly committed to the band. You will be spending an awful lot of time together, so it is important to know that you all share the same ambition. It is this that will keep you together through any times where you don't all get along. If there are any conflicts in the band, try to resolve them before you begin. If there is anyone who is not up for it, now might be the time to gently suggest that they might want to leave the band.

Don't let one person hold the rest of you back. Most importantly, get excited and look forward to the adventure, because that is what it will be. It could change your life. Whatever happens, it will be something you will never forget.

✳ FAMOUS LAST WORDS

So you've read the book. Now it's time to put your newfound knowledge into practice. Who knows where it may take you? If you've got the drive and belief to make it happen, it could take you to the top.

Good luck with your journey. Have fun, but keep your eye on the prize. And don't worry if things don't happen quite as fast as you would like. Unless you get a lucky break, the success you seek will probably take a while to achieve. Although they may appear to come from nowhere, most big name bands have a history of hard work behind them. If it helps, remind yourself that Elbow were together for seven years before they released their first EP.

If you do ever hit the big time, try to keep your feet on the ground. The music industry is littered with casualties who lost their grip soon after achieving fame and fortune. Stay focussed on your music if you want your career to last. It is important to keep coming up with new material: even the biggest selling album will only keep you in the money for so long.

One last word of advice — remember to keep enjoying what you do. If you can make a living from being in a band, you are luckier than most people alive.

SAY WHAT?

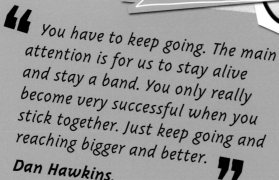

> " You have to keep going. The main attention is for us to stay alive and stay a band. You only really become very successful when you stick together. Just keep going and reaching bigger and better. "
>
> **Dan Hawkins,**
> **The Darkness and Stone Gods**

BE A QUICK EXPERT!

- Get yourselves a manager. If you want, you could try to manage the band yourself, but handing over the responsibility for the business side of things will give you more time to concentrate on the creative, fun side of being in a band.

- Record a CD to sell to fans. You could use your demo, but if you do, get some artwork made up for it and get it professionally produced.

- Think of other ways to sell your band. Design a logo or get one designed for you, then use it to sell t-shirts and other merchandise.

- Look into selling your band's music and merchandise online.

- Talk to your manager about the possibility of getting signed.

- Think about going on tour. If you don't feel confident or established enough to front a tour yourselves, consider contacting other bands and suggesting yourselves as a support act.

Write your own song!

Think of a subject that you would like to write about, then try to come up with lyrics and a melody to get your message across. If you succeed, you may have your band's first track in the bag. If you fail, you know that your band is going to need a songwriter!

Start wherever feels right to you

>> WHERE TO BEGIN? <<

There is no fixed method for writing a song. Some writers start with the lyrics, then try to come up with a tune that fits them. Others start with a melody, build a tune, then write the lyrics to fit that. If you find you have no trouble writing lyrics but cannot come up with a tune, don't panic. Many people specialise in writing lyrics alone. The same goes for tunes – many songwriters find that music comes easily to them, but that lyrics are a problem. If either of these things are true for you, work on the side you can do. You can always find a songwriting partner later on, to add what's missing.

If you get stuck, don't panic!

>> SONG STRUCTURE AND LENGTH <<

As you compose your song, tune or lyrics, think about structure. A good song should have a start (intro), verses, chorus, and an ending (outro). If you are just

working on the lyrics, you can forget about the start and ending altogether, as these are normally instrumental parts of a song. Think about the length of your song too. Most popular songs last for just three or four minutes. For more information on song anatomy see The Boffin Bit on page 22.

anything longer than this will not normally get radio play

As you write your lyrics, try to make the last words rhyme. This is not obligatory but it will make your song more catchy. It is much easier for fans to sing along to and remember songs that rhyme. Catchy songs stick in peoples' heads. They are the ones that end up being the most popular and best selling.

The part all about Song Anatomy

>> OPINIONS AND ADVICE <<

Once you have written and are happy with your song, tune or lyrics, take them to your band mates and see what they think. If you have still not yet actually formed your band, try them out with a jamming partner or a friend who is into the same sort of music as you. Take any comments or criticisms that they might have seriously. If this is your first attempt at songwriting then it is unlikely to be the best work you will ever create. If they have ideas of their own, try incorporating them into your song, tune or lyrics to see if they improve them.

Don't expect this first song to be a masterpiece – your best work is almost certainly yet to come!

A&R — artists and repertoire; a record label's A&R person or department is responsible for finding new bands and artists, and overseeing their artistic development once they have been signed

amp — short for amplifier, a piece of equipment that makes voices or instruments sound louder than they actually are

audition — in musical terms, an audition is a performance given by one person to others in order to get an idea of how that person plays or sounds. In band auditions, a potential band member usually plays along with, rather than to, the band they want to join.

biography — a person's biography is a detailed description or account of their life. A band biography (or band bio) is the story of a band.

bridge — a contrasting section of music within a song, which prepares the listener for the return of the main, original music section

cover band — a band that only plays cover songs

cover song — song performed by one band or artist that was actually first performed by somebody else

demo — short for demonstration, a demo is a recording made to give other people an idea of how a band or musician sounds

EP — stands for Extended Play; an EP is a recorded music release with somewhere between three and six different songs. In terms of length and sales price, it lies between the single and the album formats.

flyer — a small poster for handing out to people or for pinning on a notice board

hook — the part of a song most likely to catch the ear of the listener (hence the term 'catchy', as in 'catchy tune')

instrumental solo — a section of music performed by one person using one instrument, as part of a larger song. Instrumental means without words, so an instrumental solo never has lyrics.

instrumentation — the combination of musical instruments in a band

jam session — a get-together of band members or other musicians where the music played is not preplanned. Jam sessions are often used to develop songs and try out new ideas.

lyricist — a person who writes the lyrics, or words, for songs

press kit — a package of material designed to be sent to people in the press and other parts of the music industry

promotion — another word for advertising

rehearsal — a practice session, where songs that are already written and complete are played through to help band members get used to playing them

songwriter — a person who writes songs. Many songwriters write both melodies and lyrics, but the term songwriter may also be applied to a person who writes melodies alone

tribute act — a band or artist that tries to replicate another band or artist. Tribute acts usually dress and behave like the bands they are trying to replicate, as well as playing only their songs.

Rock on!

>>> INDEX <<<